# Terrariums

# Terrariums

*by John Hoke*

◄—A FIRST BOOK—►

ILLUSTRATED WITH PHOTOGRAPHS

FRANKLIN WATTS, INC./New York/1972

Library of Congress Cataloging in Publication Data

Hoke, John, 1925-
    Terrariums.

    (A First book)
    SUMMARY: Discusses the ecological require-
ments of a terrarium and gives directions for building
different kinds of plant and animal terrariums.
    Bibliography: p.
    1. Terrariums—Juvenile literature. [1. Terrari-
ums] I. Title.
QH68.H65      574'.074      70-189761
ISBN 0-531-00777-4

# Contents

# Terrariums

# Introduction

The new materials that modern industry has developed for many commercial products are often equally useful to the imaginative home and school craftsman. A number of these new materials are particularly good for terrarium design and construction. Many attractive examples of unique terrariums are shown in this book, and ways they can be built are described, including ways using these new materials.

The basic ecological requirements of terrarium life are set out in broad terms to help the newly initiated to be successful in their first efforts to build terrariums. The text discusses both animal and plantlife elements useful for terrariums. Of course, what to keep in a terrarium is very much a matter of personal taste and interest, but it is helpful to have a general knowledge of what is available.

With a little experience, you may wish to devote your attentions to a special area — such as terrariums featuring only mosses. For those who want to specialize, or learn in more detail about particular aspects and types of terrariums and living materials for them, a bibliography lists other publications that will answer these needs, and a materials list gives sources of many materials mentioned in the text.

Our environment is very much on everyone's mind today. Those who live in our cities are perhaps the most concerned because the quality of life in many of our larger cities becomes drabber with each passing year. Such terms as pollution, environmental destruction, smog, congestion, oil-spills, and a host of others appear daily on the front pages of our newspapers. Most of us know what these terms mean, for these things that are spoiling our surroundings affect all of us.

Ecology is another term many of us now understand. Since ecology represents that part of science that deals with how our environment functions, it is perhaps one of the most important areas of science today. Because of our concern, ecology is now being studied in many of our schools, with emphasis being placed on observing how different forms of life grow and perpetuate themselves.

One of the more fascinating approaches to ecological understanding is helping some kind of life from a natural environment to grow in our man-made environment — in our homes, offices, or classrooms. When we succeed, we know that we have developed a working understanding of that life form's requirements. Building a functioning terrarium is one of the best ways to create a miniature environment.

The desire to bring elements of natural environment inside our homes and to care for them extends way back in time. In ancient China, keeping exotic fish in garden pools and indoors was a fine art. One person might spend a lifetime nurturing the growth of a tiny tree — kept small by a special process of careful root cutting. Known as a Ming Tree, the single small tree, long-lived and revered, was artistically set in a shallow tray and prominently displayed in the home. It might be passed down to the next generation.

An Englishman named Nathaniel Ward made early experiments with terrariums. In 1842 he completed a book, *On the Growth of Plants in Closely Glazed Cases*. To all intents and purposes, he was the first to define the terrarium in sound ecological terms — and to take a hard look at the London environment of those days. In his book he describes the effects of air pollution on plantlife growing in the city. He experimented in bringing plants to live indoors, and his special enclosures, which became known as "Wardian cases," were the forerunners of terrariums.

Nathaniel Ward's interest in terrariums began in an unusual way. In 1829, he was attempting to hatch the chrysalis of a sphynx moth. He placed it in a bottle that contained some soil, and closed the bottle.

4

After a period of time, he noted that a small fern had sprouted, and was apparently growing in complete health in the totally sealed bottle. This same plant, however, was one he knew to be unable to survive either inside the homes or out-of-doors in the London of the 1800's! Ward concluded it was because of the "fuliginous matter" in the air of London coming from the numerous "manufactories" that had been established in the city that the plant had difficulty surviving. Ward's little fern grew and lived in the tightly sealed bottle for a number of years, and set the stage for his work in building other more sophisticated sealed and semisealed cases for growing plants in an otherwise alien environment. Ultimately, his closely glazed cases were to be used extensively on sailing ships as ways to transport exotic plantlife from many parts of the world.

The word "terrarium" means "a place of earth." In most cases a terrarium is an enclosure in which many forms of plantlife and certain animals can be kept in an ecologically healthy condition. A metal-framed glass aquarium is often used for a terrarium, and serves excellently.

Growing plants in a terrarium differs from growing them in pots on a window ledge, for the terrarium offers an added important advantage. Being an enclosure, usually of clear glass or plastic, it provides a way to control the *total* environment of the life that grows in it. Plants put in pots on a window ledge are at the mercy of room temperature — and the condition of the air in the room. If the plant finds the environment adequate it will of course thrive. But should only one physical factor be inadequate — room temperature too high or low, the air too humid or dry or contaminated in some fashion — the plant will eventually perish.

In a terrarium, however, the same plant in the same room can be

5

made to thrive in luxurious health. Being essentially closed to the outside air, all the plants' living requirements are more easily attended to, and such conditions as humidity and atmospheric warmth can be controlled along with soil moisture and nutriments. Even special lamps can now be used to promote plant growth in such places as city apartments where natural light may not be available. As long ago as the 1820's, Ward experimented with growing plants in the illumination from the flame of a lamp!

## A Good Terrarium Is a
## Functioning Ecosystem

At the heart of any terrarium is its unique ability to provide a fairly complete and controlled environment for the life it contains. Ecologically speaking, this means it will provide all the physical factors the life depends upon, without any one of which the life inside could not thrive.

If the atmosphere inside a terrarium is to be controlled, the terrarium will need to be virtually sealed from the outside atmosphere. If the most important condition is one of air humidity, the terrarium will need to be constructed of materials such as aluminum and glass, for those materials will not be affected by moisture.

If soil moisture must also be high, the aquarium type will in all probability be the best choice — with a glass cover to keep the air inside equally moist. On the other hand, if the soil must not become too moist, an aquarium may not be the best choice for want of easy ways to keep the soil drier than the air above it.

The important thing to determine before designing a terrarium is the basic set of living requirements that must be provided in the finished terrarium. It is best first to learn about the life forms you wish to keep — from friends who have successfully kept such life in a terrarium, as well as from published information. From orchid growing to keeping salamanders, there is plenty to read about the subject. If you care about the life you wish to support in a terrarium — and want to avoid the disappointment of failure — do your "homework" first. Once you have learned which basic environmental requirements are called for, and know the ways you will provide for and control each of them, you will then be on the right track to start designing and building a terrarium.

7

A well-built terrarium designed to provide basic environmental requirements will be able to house any life forms that share the need for those requirements. In this way a terrarium becomes an ecosystem, with a community made up of a certain environment and the life that grows in it. A "niche" is what ecologists call a life form's home in an ecosystem. The *ideal* terrarium is one so complete as regards its ability to attend to all the needs of the life forms it contains, as to allow you to sit back and observe it — and not have to work with it in any way! In many cases this is not always possible, nor desirable. But an attempt should be made to approach this self-sustaining situation.

## Basic Types
## of Terrariums

Given the objective that every terrarium should be as complete an ecosystem as practical, there are three general categories: the totally closed system, the partially closed case, and the vivarium.

## THE TOTALLY
## CLOSED SYSTEM

In this type of terrarium, once the life system has been set up with its basic soil and the plantlife to be grown in the system, the container is closed. In this situation, the moisture trapped in the system is recycled indefinitely — going into the soil from condensation, and back into the air through the plantlife that draws upon it as it grows. Light provides the plantlife's energy and the plants derive growth-support nutriments from the soil in which they are planted. As the plant ages and drops leaves and other parts, the decomposing bacteria and other microorganisms in the soil thrive on the decaying life, and return the nutrients to the soil for reuse in the cycle. With the continued presence of light, the cyclical process continues indefinitely.

## THE PARTIALLY
## CLOSED CASE

This kind of terrarium is used where access to the case is desired for trimming the plants, and perhaps where the addition of animal life

may be attempted. Even though the container can be opened, the ecosystem may still be fairly complete from a plantlife point of view. Whatever animal life is added, however, may need food from an outside source that is either not provided by the system or is provided in too little quantity. Snails, salamanders, anoles (a small lizard — the American chameleon), or *small* turtles are examples of animals that will do well in a terrarium. The snails and perhaps the salamanders (if few in number) may be able to care for themselves, without upsetting the plant-animal balance, but the anoles and small turtles will probably need to be provided food to meet their needs, unless the system is extremely large.

With the addition of animal life, the system's requirements of course become more complicated — the more so the *smaller* the system. But even though the enclosure needs opening from time to time to add mealworms, worms, or what have you to feed the animal life, it remains a fairly complete ecosystem so long as the plantlife, light, water, and decomposition process is flourishing. It will not have to be cleaned, after the fashion of a cage, where you have to care for all the animal's needs. In short, if you do not need to *clean* the system — if you are only called upon to add some food item from time to time, and replace moisture loss — it can be said to be a partially functioning ecosystem.

## VIVARIUM: A TERRARIUM HOME FOR ANIMAL LIFE

A stray salamander or two in a terrarium does not change its type, but if you add a fair amount of animal life to a terrarium, it will become a vivarium, supporting plant and animal life. When you add several animals to a terrarium, you will probably have to supplement their diet by adding a morsel of food from time to time, specifically for them. But no less so than with a terrarium, every effort should be made to keep all living things and physical elements in balance. If you find that the vivarium does not stay clean naturally, then you probably have too much animal life present for the system to support. You will have to decrease the animal population if you want the terrarium to stay in balance and be maintenance free.

A marked contributor to balanced life in a terrarium with animal life present is the dryland hermit crab. This little creature, like its

ocean salt-pond counterpart, lives in the discarded shells of snails —
changing to a larger one when it outgrows the one it is in. In a terrarium, crabs forage about feeding on almost everything they find discarded by the other life in the system. The dryland hermit crab is to
the terrarium, particularly the vivarium, what the catfish is to the
aquarium: In feeding upon refuse, it markedly helps keep things clean.
If only small dryland hermit crabs are used, they will never interfere
with other animal life in the system, or damage the plants. They are
comical little creatures which, in addition to their vital housecleaning
chores, provide activity that is amusing to observe as they forage about
in search of scraps of food, or a new "home" to explore and move

13

into. A few extra larger shells should be in the terrarium with the crabs. Pet stores sometimes sell these crabs. A source for them is given in the materials list.

It is well here to point out the importance of having a ready and constant supply of food for the animal life you keep in a terrarium. While many pet stores sell mealworms for feeding lizards and turtles, they may not offer them in constant supply. You may have to raise your own mealworms, or earthworms for the turtles, in a culture set up in a separate box, or purchase them from a mail-order source. The materials list includes a few places that mail them — along with earth-worm cocoons. The bibliography lists publications that describe ways to raise these foods items.

Of the three types of terrariums, the totally closed system is best attempted with plantlife whose life span can be carried out in the closed container (not outgrowing it) and the only animal life contained is primarily the microscopic life that lives in the soil and plays part of the vital decomposition role of the life cycle that takes place inside. If the system is small — aquarium-sized or less — the addition of larger animal life poses problems. True, a snail or two may live a long time but little else will find a niche adequate for all its needs — particularly if any reproduction of the animal takes place.

The second, partially closed, system lends itself better to the addition of larger than microscopic animal life. Having access to the system, you can experiment with the balance between plant and animal life. The same collection of life established in a larger terrarium — one as large as a table, for instance — will prove to be more stable. Since there is a greater abundance of each life form, the whole system is slower to respond to imbalances that may occur from time to time. This prevents catastrophies from occurring before you can discover such problems and correct them.

14

# TERRARIUMS: SMALL, MEDIUM, AND LARGE

Another valid classification that is useful to consider when planning a terrarium is the size. If but a few plants are to be kept, and they remain physically small throughout their life, a pint-sized container may do excellently. If you wish to create a slice of the forest floor, however, with virtually all its plants and some smaller animal life, a very much larger system must be built.

One must always remember that each life form can survive only if *all* of its physical requirements are met — and it can find its niche in the system. For example, it would take a terrarium bigger than your house to contain a tree — with birds, mice, deer, and the many other life forms found in and on the forest floor. So it is important to set bounds to your ambitions: A terrarium of such size for such life is best left to municipal arboretums that can afford to build such large systems.

A tabletop terrarium is about as big a system as the average home or school can manage — and finance. One of this size is described in detail in this book. It will support a wide variety of plants, several *small* turtles, some salamanders, and perhaps a half dozen anoles, earthworms, and a few small dryland hermit crabs. It is big enough to allow varying the numbers of animal life, without serious risk of upsetting the system too soon to correct any damage. Light, water, and food for the animals are all that need to be provided. The basic growth processes of the plantlife in the terrarium is what keeps it clean.

## Requirements:
## Six Important
## Considerations

The beginning of all related life processes is light.

## LIGHT

Plants require light for their food-making process. They extract minerals from the soil, and the breakdown of plant materials replaces these minerals. This exchange with the soil is the basic process that must function well in a terrarium in order for all life in it to thrive. While all green-leafed plants require light, some need direct sunlight, while others thrive only in the shadowy light like that beneath a forest canopy. And many plants can only thrive if they experience cyclical breaks in the illumination such as those provided by day and night.

Artificial light gardening has become a well-developed field today, and you can now obtain a variety of special lamps that provide the different kinds of illumination needed to grow plants of all kinds. (See materials list for sources.)

Much has been written to guide you in the choices of light needed to grow certain plants. If you have collected your own plants, however, you can pretty well guess which ones require direct sunlight, and which must live in shade — because of the locations where you found them. The suppliers of the special plant-growth lamps will provide you with data that will guide you when you are in doubt.

Smaller forest-floor plants usually require incident light, that is, light reflected from another object, and may well perish if exposed to direct sunlight. Many field grasses and flowers, swamp plants — and

16

plants such as corn — may germinate and grow for a while in indirect — filtered — light, but many will not mature if they do not receive enough direct sunlight. Remembering where you got a specific plant is important — particularly if you have not yet identified it but wish to put it right into a terrarium.

## SOIL CONDITION

The next most important consideration is *the kind of soil* a given plant needs in order to grow. Its chemical makeup — whether it is acid or base, how tightly packed it is, how much organic matter is present with the inorganic parts of the soil — is an important consideration for each kind of rooted plant. There are some kinds of plants that should *not* be planted in soil: Some kinds of orchids and similar plants grow on other plants and collect or create their own soil in and about their roots over a period of time, while other plants are simply suspended on host plants and do not depend on soil in any way.

Soil is composed of both decayed organic materials and inorganic matter. Insofar as terrarium culture is concerned, soil is often broken down into three components — *humus, leaf mold,* and *loam.* Humus is partially decayed organic matter that includes both animal and vegetative material. This is the rich brown or black matter that you find in well-worked compost piles. Leaf mold is similar matter, but is primarily composed of decomposed vegetation (leaves, etc.). Loam is the claylike and largely inorganic material that is hard caked when dry, and pastelike when wet.

Selecting the proper soil is again a question of reading about the needs of each kind of plant you wish to keep — or removing and

17

studying a portion of the soil in which you find a plant you wish to grow in a terrarium.

Needless to say, if you put one kind of soil in your terrarium, and illuminate it with only one kind of light, you can only successfully cultivate those plants that will grow in those light and soil conditions. Strangers to your community of plants may thrive for a short period of time, but it is too much to ask that they thrive in as healthy a state as those plants for which your terrarium matches their natural home.

## AIR AND SOIL MOISTURE

The third important consideration is *air and soil moisture*. Plants that root in a wet water bog or swamp will not grow in dry sand. And, conversely, cacti and other desert plants will do badly in very moist soil. The water in the air — humidity — is equally important. Again, if only one condition of moisture prevails in your terrarium, it will only be able to support those plants that require or can endure that moist an environment: It is a tall order to build a single terrarium in which to keep both cacti and mosses. The mosses prefer a relatively moist, low-illumination environment that is cool. Cacti are used to a drier sandy soil and atmosphere, bright sun, and daytime warmth.

## TEMPERATURE

The fourth consideration is *temperature*. There are plants that grow well in very warm and humid (or dry) climate, while others thrive at near-freezing temperatures. Some plants do best when their growth seasonally experiences a period of warm climate followed by a number of weeks of cooler weather. This leads to the next consideration.

## VARIATIONS: SEASONAL AND LIGHT

The fifth consideration is *seasonal and illumination variation*. Many plants, like other living things, need periods of seasonal rest, just as they need the day-night break in the illumination that enables them photosynthetically to process light, gases, and the soil nutrients and moisture that support their growth. While each plant's degree of sensitivity to these cycles varies — some can be pushed for rapid growth's sake — there are those that must experience these seasonal and light cycles exactly as they exist in their natural environment if they are to thrive. Unless you are in a position to program these requirements with special clocks or careful attention on your part, you may wish to avoid such plants until you are quite experienced.

## CLEANLINESS

The last consideration is *terrarium housecleaning*. The best indication that a terrarium is functioning successfully is that it is keeping itself clean naturally. In the natural environment important decomposition processes are at work all the time. These processes are just as important in the balanced terrarium. And your nose is about the best instrument you have on hand to determine if these processes are at work

19

in your terrarium. If the terrarium is clean, it will *smell* clean — even if it contains some animal life.

Microorganisms soon establish themselves in the soil of the terrarium — thriving on the waste products that all the living things in the system drop to the soil. In the balanced terrarium dead plant matter and the droppings from any animal life that is present are soon absorbed. If these dead materials and animal droppings are quickly absorbed, they will not smell offensive — and their disappearance is proof that the decomposition processes are in balance and functioning well. If there is too much of something for the decomposers to handle, the system will soon smell offensive, and may begin to break down unless these excesses are taken care of quickly.

Balance is a basic condition of a well-planned, well-functioning terrarium, regardless of its size. And since smaller systems are quicker to respond to too much or too little of something, even more care must be taken in selecting the things that are to live in the system.

In general, fewer living and nonliving components should be put in a very small system — which can involve as few as a single plant, its own chosen soil, the right amount of moisture, the right kind of light, and the proper temperature. By learning about their basic requirements you will be able to identify which of those living things you wish to keep share common physical requirements. While you may wish to include life that does not exactly fit into the physical requirements package you have created, knowing about the problem in advance will alert you to what may be giving you trouble, if something goes wrong.

These are the important basic elements that require your attention when you decide to create and cultivate a terrarium.

# Materials:
# Living and Natural


## SOIL

A jar with some soil and a lone plant in it can be called a terrarium. But even here you can be imaginative. A unique container — a goblet, exotic bottle, or what have you — can add a great deal. But first, you must prepare a soil base for any plants you select. There are several basic techniques for providing a good soil foundation.

In most cases, soil out of the yard is not likely to be the best choice for the kinds of plants you will probably plant in a terrarium. Soil out of the yard is all too often dense and muddy when wet. Until you are ready to specialize in soil mixtures tailored to the needs of special plants, it is best to start with a standardized mix of soil ingredients. Such a standard mix can be created by using equal portions of a good rich soil, coarse sand, and the compost that is found in a year-old moist pile of leaves. These should be evenly mixed together, and moist — but not wet.

Many garden shops sell sterilized potting soil in packages. This soil has been baked, or otherwise processed so that no unwanted molds or other plant-damaging life are present. True, vital decomposing life is also missing, but this life will soon develop. These packaged soils are ideal to begin with, particularly in urban areas where you cannot easily find the natural ingredients nearby.

In preparing the soil foundation in the terrarium it is important to avoid packing it down in such a way that it can become hard and claylike with successive watering. To insure that the soil remains

21

loose — and a water level does not settle in it — a loose layer of coarse gravel should be put in the container, on which the soil is then placed. A piece of plastic screen on top of the base layer of gravel can be used to keep soil from filling air spaces in the gravel.

The soil foundation in a terrarium can be a flat plane, or with a little imagination you can create steps and terraces by the skillful use of rocks in the soil.

The only thing to be wary of in building a tiered floor for your terrarium is to be sure that the soil of each layer you create is in over-all contact with the soil of other layers and not separated in any way by any rock ledges you create. By having all the soil in the terrarium in contact — "bridged" to join layers above and below — you can be more assured that soil moisture is uniform. If soil on a particular ledge were cut off from contact with soil in the bottom, it might dry out even though the soil elsewhere was damp.

From the standpoint of terrarium building, rocks are largely an aesthetic consideration. Providing a good basic soil meets the nutritional needs of the plants. There are several exceptions of course. Certain kinds of lichens grow on rock itself. Lichens are a plant that is really two plants — fungus and algae — living together in what is known as symbiosis. Two organisms living together like this serve each other's needs in one or another important way. In this case, the fungus provides the water and mineral nutrients the alga needs, while the alga provides any carbohydrates its fungus partner needs.

Since lichens found on rock are slow to develop, choices of rock might best be made from those that already have a patch of lichen on them. But in the terrarium, lichens will do best if not shielded from sun altogether, or kept too moist.

## PLANTS:
## BASIC NEEDS IN A
## TERRARIUM

Plants can now be set in the soil, and here is where your artistic lean-
ings can be given full sway. Try to avoid overcrowding. Plants need
their fair share of space just as other living creatures do. You can use
gravel and small slabs of attractive rock or moss to separate plantings.
Handle the plants gently, for their root systems are easily injured. Set
each in place, and sweep — do not pack — soil up around their roots.
If they are plants you collected yourself, and you dug them up with
a clump of their own soil, they can be easily set in place with their
own soil around their roots. This will insure their having the particular
soil mix they need, regardless of the basic soil you used for the terrarium soil foundation.

Planting a terrarium can be an easy, quickly done task if the container is large and easy to work in. Planting in a bottle or other
narrow-neck container is another proposition, and it can be just as
challenging a task as building a ship in a bottle. It will call for plant-
handling tools made of wood slivers, coat-hanger wire, and whatever
else the inventive mind can think of for building a garden through a
keyhole. But the results will be the more rewarding, for this will add
to its charm. Those who look at it will be just as impressed with the
accomplishment as they would be with an intricate ship model built
inside a bottle.

If the terrarium is to be a home only for plants the basic prepara-
tion is completed once the plants are in place. They will shape themselves with time. Be sure that they receive enough light of the right

kind — and special attention if things do not go well at first. Before the terrarium is covered, or corked, make sure the correct amount of moisture is present. The moist mix of soil is usually enough, if when handled it does not leave much visible liquid moisture on your hands. If you have bought prepared packaged soil, the amount of water to add to it is usually part of the instructions that come with the soil. When in doubt, a little less water is better than too much. Before closing up a system which is to be totally sealed, cover it temporarily for a few days and watch it to see that plants do not wilt for want of soil moisture.

If water needs to be added, spray it on the plants with an atomizer bottle (see materials list), or similar misting method. It is best not to soak the soil with unknown volumes of water. This can encourage growth of fungi and molds which, once established, are not dispelled simply by drying out the container. They may respond to special preparations, but in many cases they do so much damage before they are removed that you have to start all over with fresh soil and plants. It is best to use water sparingly.

When the terrarium is closed, moisture may condense on the glass sides from time to time. A little such moisture is good and indicates there is adequate moisture in the system, provided the run-off does not puddle in an obviously water-saturated soil!

The terrarium will need light, but it is best not exposed to daily direct sunlight long enough to raise its inside temperature much over 70° F. (See materials list for thermometers.) If your terrarium features mosses and other forest floor vegetation, it should not be exposed to direct sunlight at all. It will thrive in any part of the room where it will be cool. The indirect light coming through the windows will be sufficient for the plants.

24

Once you feel the terrarium has been properly established, leave it alone to settle down. In time, the real measure of your success will be that you can proudly proclaim to admiring friends, "I haven't had the lid off since I made it!"

## PLANTS: WHICH KINDS FOR WHICH TERRARIUM?

What plants will grow in different soil mixtures has much to do with their origins. For example, cacti have evolved to live in arid places that are often devoid of rich soil. To the other extreme, swamp plants and some bog plants can root and thrive in enriched silt (soil composed of sedimentary materials). Most flowering plants require a fairly rich soil. Those that need full sunlight can manage in even hard-textured soil such as that found in open meadows. But the harder and less nutritious the soil, the scraggier this vegetative cover grows. This of course is why the farmer periodically fertilizes the soil or plants a special "soil-restoring" crop such as clover, which will alter the basic nature of the soil. Forest floor plants thrive in a soil that is rich because of the breakdown of leaf vegetation dropped from the overhead canopy. The air beneath the canopy is humid, for the trees release — and hold below — considerable water as a part of their growth process.

While there is not space in this book just to list the great numbers of plants that can be put in different kinds of terrariums, comparing a few examples with respect to their soil, illumination, and moisture needs will serve as a guide in deciding what kind of terrarium you would like to create. The following divisions are quite arbitrary. There are many plants that live *in* bordering areas between desert, fields, swampland, meadows, woodland forests, etc. But the breakdowns that follow will help you understand the interrelationship between the various living requirements of different plants.

## SUNNY AND DRY

Visions of the western plains and deserts come to mind for the sunny and dry setting. In a tray of sandy soil — or open-mouthed jars and goblets — cacti and sun-loving plants will do well on a shelf inside a brightly lit window.

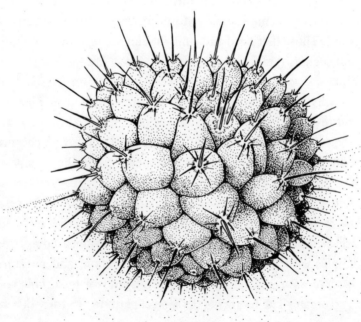

CACTUS

Desert cacti can be grown along with desert and prairie succulents, agaves, and aloes. The materials list gives a source for seeds of both cacti and prairie wild flowers and plants that can be bought by mail for use in such a terrarium. You may be hard put to find arid-land plants if you live in a city far away from desert areas. Many florists sell potted cacti already grown to attractive heights. In setting up a terrarium using potted cacti, it is often best to set the pots in which they were bought right into the tray.

These arid-area plants do need light waterings with a misting sprayer, and some soil dampening, but above all, do not drench arid-area plants.

ALOE

Almost any meadow or pasture plant — and of course a great variety of greenhouse and flower-shop potted plants — will thrive in an open-top terrarium that is placed near a well lit, southern-exposure window. Soil should be moist and it need not be overly rich in humus, so long as it does not contain so much loam as to allow the soil to cake and get hard.

Some lichens on rock, or pieces of wood, sand, or soil, will live in a community of smaller field flowering plants. "British Soldiers" and "Pyxie Cups" (*Fruticose lichens*) are quite attractive, but are best transplanted with whatever soil they are found on, to insure they obtain their own special soil requirements.

Many wild flowers will grow from seeds or can be transplanted into an open sunny terrarium — the only problem will be to select small species that will not grow up and out the top of the terrarium (unless

LICHEN

LICHEN

that is what you want!). Yellow clover is very pretty. If you live in a city, many small-leafed plants can be found growing in cracks in the sidewalk and in the brickwork of walls. They, too, will thrive in an open sunlit terrarium.

Plants that like a lot of sunlight pose a problem living in a terrarium lighted from a nearby window. They tend to lean toward the light as they grow. People have long solved this problem with potted plants by simply rotating them from time to time. This is hard to do with a terrarium — unless you place it on a large lazy susan tray.

You can of course grow the kinds of plants requiring sunlight with special fluorescent lights, but it takes quite a concentration of lights to do it. If the lights are not sufficiently intense, many of these open field plants will grow tall and stringy — reaching for better illumination. And so window sunlight is best for these, with a daily rotation of the terrarium to keep them growing straight up. Plant-growth lamps are therefore best left for nurturing plants that require less light.

29

## SUNNY AND DAMP

Swamp vegetation comes to mind, here. The thought of swamp plants in a terrarium may strike one as an odd choice, but many wetlands plants are very attractive. And an interesting experiment can be performed when making a swampland terrarium.

In the dead of winter, many swampy areas are iced over. Sometimes the water level may have dropped, exposing muckland "bottom," now quite hard and frozen. Using a pick or hatchet, you can cut out a block of this iced muck — to fit a tray, aquarium, or planter, and

bring it indoors. In the instant spring warmth of your home or school-room, under a lamp, it will soon thaw and quickly come to life. A special lamp known as a "sun bowl" (materials list) lends itself ideally to this experiment.

31

Cattails, arrowheads, and many of the myriad of swamp-bottom plants will put out shoots — so long as the slab you cut is kept thoroughly wet under about half an inch of water. If you brought in your slice of swamp in the middle of December, you will have upward of six inches of growth on it by the time spring comes. This is an excellent way to observe spring's effect upon the wetlands.

CATTAIL                    ARROWHEAD

From this point on, the kinds of plants most often thought of for use in terrariums predominate. Beneath the sun-shading and moisture-containing canopy of woods and forests exists an entire system of forest floor plantlife. While some of these plants thrive best where the sun peeks through the canopy for a time each day, particularly plants that live in the border between woods and open fields, the balance derive all the light they need from shaded illumination.

In general, the forest floor soil contains considerable humus and decaying leaf material — sometimes on and gradually mixed in with loose sandy loam beneath it. The soil is often quite dry except following a drenching rain, but the air above it is usually somewhat humid. Where ground water is trapped in lows, or where clay is present beneath the surface, the results will be bog conditions and a damper soil.

A good general soil base for a woodland terrarium can be made by mixing equal parts of humus, leaf mold, and a filler of course sand or pumice rock (available from many garden suppliers). A gravel subfloor covered with a screen goes in first, on which the mixed soil is then placed. When plants are finally added, it is still best to plant them with a bit of the soil that surrounded their roots when they were found in the woods.

Ferns, mosses, and selaginellas are ideal plants to represent in a woodland terrarium, for they will not need exposure to direct sunlight, and indeed should not be allowed to become warmer than 75° F. All will do well in a closed terrarium, which includes gardens in bottles, brandy snifters, and "worlds under a dome." Among the ferns, members of the *Asplenium* and *Adiantum* families will grow in a wide choice of containers. For very small containers, the *Pteris* offers very

33

attractive delicate foliage. In larger terrariums and cases, smaller specimens of *Belchnum* ferns can be included.

Mosses found in sheets or patches on the forest floor make fine carpets to provide space or green-spans between individual mosses and plants that grow vertically. One of those that provide carpeting is *Leucobryum glaucum* — it has an almost miniature grasslike quality. *Dicranum flagellare,* though shaggier, can also provide carpeting for the terrarium.

Selaginellas and small seedlings of leafed plants can be planted between the moss-carpeted areas. Among the selaginellas, *S. uncinata* and *S. emmeleana* develop graceful leafage to complement the moss-banks and ferns. Partridge berry (*Mitchella repens*), Pipsissewa (*Chimaphila* sp.), and rattlesnake plantain (*Goodyera pubescens*) —

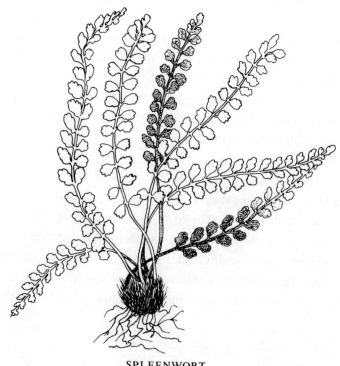

34

SPLEENWORT

a member of the orchid family — do well tucked in among clumps of moss.

Getting a good balance of moisture between the subsurface soil and the air above can be a touchy undertaking. Too much soil *and* air moisture can bring much grief from unwanted fungus and mold development. When the terrarium is first planted, the soil should be loose and damp — but not so damp as to leave obvious wetness on your hands. When the enclosure is finally covered, condensation should appear on the sides, but not so much as to run constantly down the sides. If it does, leave the top off for a day to release some of the moisture. (If seedling plants seem to suffer from dryness, drop a bit of water with an eyedropper on their roots to keep them alive, while the top is off.) When the closed system exhibits some fogging of the glass, and the mosses look their greenest, you are home free.

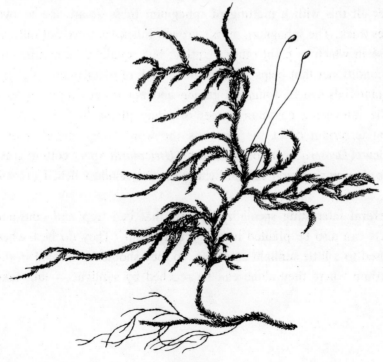

MOSS

Plants that live near the water's edge of woodland streams and in shadowy bog bottoms are featured here. The soil these plants live in is mostly rich in humus and leaf mold, and quite damp. Some bog plants thrive in soil that is in standing water.

In spite of the unappealing sounding conditions a bog or marsh presents, a host of very attractive and unusual plants, including several species of mosses, thrive in these conditions. And to have them live in a room at your home or school, these wet conditions must be created in their terrarium home.

A good general soil base for a bog terrarium begins with a layer of half-inch sized gravel covered with a plastic screen. On this goes a half to one-inch thick mix of small granule or crushed activated carbon or charcoal and fine aquarium gravel (larger mesh than sand). Cover all this with a matting of sphagnum moss about one to two inches thick. The sphagnum moss's growth functions serve not only as a base in which to plant other plantlife, but equally as a continuous soil conditioner that helps support the growth of other plants. (These soil materials can be found in garden and aquarium supply stores.)

The interesting common names of many plants that do well in a bog terrarium offset the drabness the word "bog" might imply: Sundew (*Drosera* sp.), bladderwort (*Utricularia* sp.), cotton grass (*Eriophorum* sp.), and certain lichens such as reindeer lichen (*Usnea* sp.).

Several interesting specialized plants that can trap and consume insects can also be planted in a bog terrarium. (They do best when exposed to a little sunlight each day, so they should be located in the terrarium where they alone can be reached by sunlight — but take

36

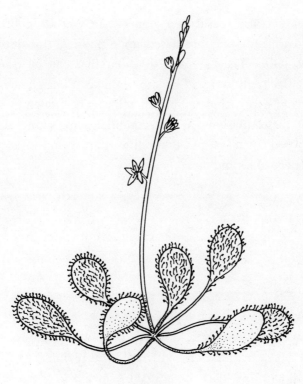

SUNDEW

care the whole terrarium does not reach a temperature of 70–75° F. as a result.) Among these are the pitcher plant (*Sarracenia purpurea*) and the Venus's flytrap (*Dionaea muscipula*). While they can be fed and will digest insects (or small pieces of meat) they do not need to be fed such a diet. It makes a good show for a doubting friend, but is not vital to the plant's well-being.

Every plant form you encounter will find its niche somewhere between "sunny and dry" and "shady and damp." These divisions

37

will be particularly useful as a guide when you are collecting plants on a field trip, for they are based upon physical conditions you can easily recognize. They are also divisions that can be translated into the particular terrarium you choose to make. Your choice of building materials and supporting equipment will also be guided by the physical nature of these divisions. Where conditions are sunny and dry, you can use wood for trays, but if conditions are going to be very damp, you may need glass and metal.

COTTONGRASS

## Containers:
## Any Shape Will Do

A great many terrariums have been built inside a container originally made for some other purpose. Today, with clear plastic added to glass as a material for making containers, the choice is even greater. A terrarium container can also be designed and built on one's own, an added challenge offering limitless design possibilities.

Small, medium, and large were the terms we used earlier to classify sizes of terrariums. Another aspect to consider is that terrariums can be made *in* a container or can be gardens *under* a cover. In either case, the environment is enclosed and protected.

The following section will deal with different ways of building terrariums in enclosed containers of many kinds, and terrariums that are constructed on trays under covers. All the materials used can be bought at local shops or from the firms listed in the materials list. Generally speaking the costs are nominal for each of the systems shown, and the tools in the average home workshop are all that are needed to aid in building these systems. In keeping with the size classification of small, medium, and large, let us start small.

## SMALL TERRARIUMS

The equipment needs for a small terrarium are quite modest; i.e. a container, some potting soil, a *few* small forest floor plants, and a cap for the container.

For good visibility, the container should be of clear glass and should be well cleaned. Since the amount of soil used will be small, it can be picked up with the few plants you collect and filled out in the

39

container if necessary with potting soil. For purposes of illustration, a single plant and several samples of moss are used in the picture sequence in which, step by step, a terrarium is built in a brandy snifter.

A brandy snifter has long been a favorite container for a terrarium, for it is easy to use. If you have a large snifter, you can add more plants. If you want to close it up, place a piece of glass over it, or stretch plastic food film over the top. If the plants you choose, however, prefer more air and sunlight, leave the top open.

*A brandy snifter and the materials to be used to plant a garden in it. From left, rocks, two paper cups of gravel and activated carbon, a dish of prepared soil, and a circular plastic screen to separate the soil from the gravel and carbon. To the right of the brandy snifter stem are mosses and other forest floor plants to be planted in the prepared soil base.*

*With the gravel in place on the bottom of the snifter, spread the activated carbon on top.*

41

*Push a piece of plastic foam through a hole in the center of the screen. This foam will serve as a wick to redistribute any water that collects in the subsoil of carbon and gravel. One piece of the wick should stick up almost to the top surface of the soil. Place the circular screen on top of the gravel and carbon. Put some small flat rocks on top of the screen and on the blades of the wick.*

Pour the soil in place onto the screen and wick, and begin planting. If several tiers are to be created, do the first tier planting completely before moving on to the next. After setting in leafed plants (with clusters of their own soil, wherever possible), carpet the open areas with layers of moss or flat stones. A circle of small stones — on the first tier — is all it takes to form a pot for the second tier's soil. (Here's where the foam wick helps to carry subsoil water up to this second tier.) Plant the second level as you did the first. A typewriter eraser brush makes a fine tool for moving dirt around — and for sweeping away dirt that sticks to the glass side of the snifter.

43

After a light watering with a squirt bottle (leaf plant clusters should have an extra portion of water near their roots) cover the snifter: a plastic container cover — or piece of glass — can be placed over the top. This will close in the atmosphere enough so that only an occasional watering will be necessary.

*If things look uneven and scraggly at first, don't worry. Under a growth lamp, or after several days' rotation in window light (not direct sunlight!), leaves will straighten out. If some plants grow too high, just snip them back with shears. In time, harmony will occur among the plants — and your terrarium will grow more attractive with each passing day.*

45

## MEDIUM-SIZE TERRARIUMS

### AN AQUARIUM TERRARIUM

Planting in an aquarium is little different from planting in a small bottle. It is easier because you are working through a large top, and because it is larger, you can add a great deal more plantlife and materials such as rocks and ornamental figurines. You begin with a soil base such as was described earlier (gravel, plastic screen, and soil). Whether you enclose the aquarium under a sheet of glass, of course, depends upon whether high air humidity is required — such as for a woodland terrarium or even more so, a bog terrarium.

Under this medium-size category, let us explore an interesting form of tabletop terrarium that takes advantage of the many kinds of plastic covers now being made.

### WORLD UNDER A DOME

A terrarium built on a tray is the basic design element of this kind of terrarium. Many small plants, including mosses from the forest floor, will thrive in this kind of enclosure since their humid climate is maintained under a covering dome of plastic or glass. A source of incident light for energy, and an occasional mist-watering with an atomizer or spray bottle to replace moisture loss whenever the enclosure is opened for close observation, are about all the attention the finished system needs. A "world under a dome" becomes, in effect, an attractive exhibit of forest floor plantlife in an unusual housing. Materials for making domelike enclosures are available in wide varieties of sizes and shapes. They range from large, hemispherical domes-on-trays used in restaurants and as cake covers, to inverted plastic drinking tumblers. To make it easier to view all sides of the terrarium, larger units can be constructed on lazy susan turntables. Then they may be easily turned occasionally for all-round viewing and to make sure all sides are evenly exposed to their light source.

Plants that are ideally suited to this domelike environment include such forest floor plants as mosses, small ferns, partridge berries, lichens, and rattlesnake plantain. The plants should be arranged on the tray so they will efficiently occupy the space and look natural and attractive from all sides.

Selecting a tray and transparent cover to meet any size and shape requirement can be accomplished by visiting local grocery and hardware stores. Many glass or plastic products lend themselves to terrarium use, but you will have to look at them with your goal in mind to recognize them. For example, there are a number of glass canisters in varying sizes sold to hold cookies, flour, sugar, etc., that have slip-on covers of plastic. Turned upside down, so that the glass "bottom" becomes the terrarium top, and the plastic cover is now the tray bottom, you have an ideal enclosure for this kind of terrarium.

The size of a "world under a dome" can range from clear plastic drinking glasses (again, upside down) to cake covers — complete with matching tray. Basic to a really large attractive "world under a dome" is a hemispherical dome of plastic. Such an item will not likely be found in local stores, and for large systems it will be more expensive than cake covers of similar size. But for school use, or for the home horticulturist who wants a unique hemispherical terrarium, its cost is not beyond consideration. A source of such large domes, in various sizes, is provided in the materials list.

Some of these commercially made domes will fit on a wide assortment of circular trays sold in many stores. Among these is a line of lazy susan trays that rotate easily on bearings built into the trays.

These trays are ideal platforms for an attractive rock pile on which to plant the rock-ledge moss garden described earlier.

If you wish to make a very small covered garden under a plastic drinking tumbler, for example, the tiered ledges will be quite small. Try to purchase a plastic tumbler that comes with a snap-fit cover. It is on this you will first construct the tier in which to set small plants.

*The world under a dome begins with a framework to build upon. The many tiers can be created with rock alone — or by using plastic boxes cemented together.*

*Thoroughly clean slabs of rock, then cement them together or to the plastic boxes. (Silastic rubber may be used as a cement — it requires up to several days to dry — or epoxy cement, which dries faster.)*

Scotch tape spools, parts of pill vials, and other small plastic scrap are used as separators for single pieces of small circular slabs of stone (each smaller than the slab below it). The parts of the pile should be cemented together with silastic rubber in such a way that the plastic used to separate each stone slab will not be visible when the plants are put in place.

49

When the frame is thoroughly dry, place coarse sand on each tier, then soil on top of that. Cut pieces of moss to fit between tiers. Tuck leaf plants and ferns in between the pieces of moss.

*The finished garden with the cover added becomes a world under a dome.*

For such a small garden under a dome, you must select your plants with care. Plants that could outgrow the container should of course be avoided.

Big or small, taking care of a world under a dome that features mosses and other forest floor plants is relatively simple. If you remove the cover to inspect the plants more closely, or to show it to a friend, be sure not to forget to put it back. If condensation fails to appear shortly after putting the cover back in place you may want to spray a little water on the plants to restore the moisture lost when the dome was open.

These examples of covered tray terrariums are the kind ideally suited for housing small gardens in a closed or semisealed environment. Like gardens planted in glass containers, such as goblets, jars, and the

*For those who would like to avoid the expense of a large heavy plastic dome, it is possible to "blow your own dome" using a low-cost rigid film plastic (see materials list for sources). Making the dome is an interesting manual art project for school — or the home workshop enthusiast. The domes can be made in almost any shape or to fit the lazy susans found in hardware stores.*

*The materials needed to blow covers are simple and cost very little. The long roll to the left in the picture is the butyrate plastic, 15 mils (.015") thick, the kind used to "blister-pack" small commercial products. Next is a rubber-cushioned plywood base plate that fits with any of the plywood templates shown next. Holes have been cut in them to form the shape of the dome. To the right is the oven. It consists of two layers of 8 to 10 feet of corrugated shipping cardboard, stapled together. Aluminum foil has been cemented to the smooth side of the cardboard sandwich. In front of the three templates is a porcelain light fixture and a power cord. There is a heating element in the fixture. An oven thermometer is required to control the temperature. To the right is an aquarium air pump and tubing. Aquarium plastic tubing can be used, but rubber air tubing stands up better in the heat. In the foreground are four trays and domes blown to fit them.*

like, they can be left to themselves. Aside from light reaching them through their transparent container, and an occasional watering, their requirements are attended to by the activities carried out almost entirely inside their miniature enclosed world.

The base plate is made of good quality ⅜" plywood that is perfectly flat. Then ⅜" sponge rubber weather stripping is cemented on the plywood to match the edge of the hole in the template that will lie on it. The template is made of ¼" plywood.

The plastic film is sandwiched between the base and the template and fastened together with large clamps.

The wood plates create an airtight pocket between the film and the base plate. When the film is warmed sufficiently to yield to air pressure, air pumped into this pocket will make the plastic blow out through the template hole.

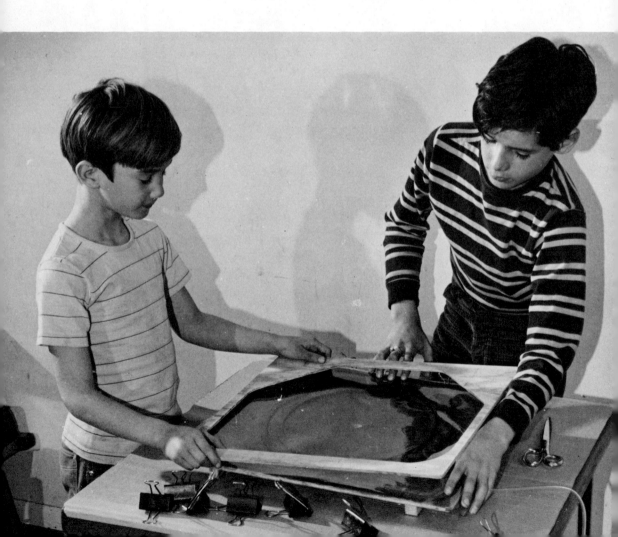

An air input fitting is made by gluing an input fitting to the back of the base plate. Holes are drilled in the fitting so air will flow through the wood block and base plate.

Two frame pieces keep the base plate flat; and two eye bolts are used to secure the base plate under the top of the cardboard oven. (Two slots are cut in the plywood top of the oven and the bolts are slipped through these slots. A coat-hanger wire is then passed through both eyes to secure the base plate.) Once the sandwich is clamped together, the tube is plugged onto the fitting and the assembly is fitted to the cover of the oven.

55

*The oven is made by setting the aluminum-foil-coated cardboard roll up on end, and enlarging it to a 2 to 3 foot diameter column. To allow viewing, a window is cut into the cardboard and covered with a piece of the plastic film.*

The template sandwich, with an oven thermometer attached, is hung from the plywood top, and the heating element is placed on the floor below. A lamp can be hung inside to improve visibility. All wires and the air tubing extend under the edge of the oven to the outside. When the oven is taped shut, the heating element is plugged into a power outlet until the oven reaches about 220° F. At this point, the air pump is turned on. So the blown dome will be uniform in shape, lots of hose should be used — all hung inside the oven wall away from the heating element. This will ensure that the air blown into the template is well warmed.

By looking through the oven window, you can decide when the dome is big enough, at which time you turn off the heater and open the oven. But keep pumping. Air shrinks as it cools, and so a head of pressure must be maintained until the plastic cools and sets.

57

Open the oven and it will soon cool. When not too hot to handle, the oven top can be lifted off and put right side up on a nearby table. When the dome is cool to the touch (pump still running), you can start taking off the clamps. Then turn off the pump, trim the edge of the plastic with shears, and you have your custom-made terrarium dome.

58

## A Cylindrical Home
## for Plants and Animals

When animal life is added to a world under a dome, or any other terrarium, the system will need more attention. True, a small salamander in a large terrarium may find all it needs in the closed system. But if all that is needed to keep a few more forms of animal life in a terrarium is a bit more care on your part, the added effort can be well worth it. Anoles will do well in some kinds of terrariums — particularly in tall, cylindrical ones. One of the most easily built systems for housing both plants and anoles uses simple plastic parts, and calls for little skill to assemble it.

The parts for this cylindrical environment are commonly found in many local stores. Which piece fits with which will depend on the kinds of plastic container lids you select for the top and bottom of this enclosure, so specific measurements for building this enclosure are not given here other than to suggest using clear acetate sheeting for the tubular sides that is at least .0075 inches (7½ mils) thick. Clear acetate sheeting in all thicknesses can be bought in most drafting supply stores.

The basic structure is a cylinder made of a single piece of acetate sheeting that nests between two identical-sized plastic container tops that serve in this case as both the top and bottom of the enclosure.

An interesting variant of the cylindrical enclosure is one that is made from a commercial lamp known as a "sun bowl" (see materials list). This lamp uses a special circular fluorescent tube designed to promote plant growth. Since the top and base of the lamp are identical in shape, it is an easy matter to fit it with a cylindrical tube of acetate cut from a sheet of 7½ mil thick stock, 9½" x 29¹¹⁄₁₆" long, to form an enclosure for plants and anoles.

*Cylinder enclosure. Top and bottom are "tops" of two 10" diameter plastic containers. Cylinder is a tube made of .0075", or thicker, drafting-store acetate sheeting — overlapped ½" and taped together with scotch tape that is adhesive on both sides (another drafting-store item).*

*Air holes are hand punched just inside the edges of the acetate tube — to line up with holes drilled in the lips of the caps.*

60

*A plastic drinking cup has been cemented in the center of the bottom in which to plant a small palm tree. Soil is spread on the floor for plants, while at least an inch of gravel rims the planting area so lizards and hermit crabs won't track up the acetate walls with their dirty feet.*

This lamp — with acetate tube — can be used as a planter for mosses and other small plants. A column of rock or rock shelves is built in the bottom of the lamp not unlike the ones built for a world under a dome, only here the pile should be taller. This variation of design calls for building a tier of plastic shelves on which small slabs of rock are cemented to hide the plastic skeleton. This structuring provides plenty of room for setting in slices of moss bank and other plantings. The finished vertically shaped garden is then enclosed by the acetate tube, which is held in place by the top and bottom of the lamp. A hole drilled through the top of the sun bowl provides a place to drip water into the garden.

When the sun bowl is used as a home for anoles — with perhaps a miniature palm tree and a baby-tears ground cover — some air should be allowed to circulate through the chamber. Several holes should be punched through the acetate tube edges. The lamp, being warm, will promote air circulation through the system by drawing air in through the bottom holes, and venting it through those at the top of the cylinder. In this use of the lamp, mealworms for the anoles (two anoles are plenty in this small enclosure) will have to be dropped in, so the hole cut in the top of the lamp housing must be fitted with a plastic plug of some sort to keep the anoles from crawling out of it. It is best to remove the glass tube from the lamp while cutting this hole.

*Cylinder container with palm tree, using a "sun bowl" for top.*

# LARGE TERRARIUMS

## TABLETOP ENVIRONMENT
## FOR PLANTS AND ANIMALS

This might best be called a twentieth-century Wardian case, for it is similar in shape, serves many similar purposes, and utilizes modern materials and control methods. As enclosures go, it can be made quite large to suit schoolroom needs and those whose interest in terrariums is great enough to warrant the cost of a large system. You will probably need the help of an adult with a project of this size.

This terrarium is designed to support both plant and animal life. It includes a warming lamp, a small blower that can be used to control inside humidity and temperature, and can accommodate a water fountain and running stream to enhance its appearance and to insure adequate humidity. These items can add to the enclosure's cost, but are mentioned here to illustrate the flexibility of enclosure design possibilities.

## PLANTING THE CASE

The 4-inch deep base of this enclosure is where all soil and plantings are placed. If the base is large enough — say 2 x 4 feet — you may want to plant a small shrub or dominant plant in the center on which anoles can climb to bask in the overhead light. This shrub is best planted in a shallow plastic container to be set into the base as a separate unit in the soil.

It is important to plan the planting layout with respect to what kinds of plants are to be used and their place in the floor of the enclosure. You can of course cover the base with plants, but some open

64

area can be created by using coarse sand or fine gravel. In the terra-rium illustrated a sandy area is shown. Part of your plan should include how you fill the space *below* the soil's surface. In many cases, except for the main or central large plant, the soil need be no more than 2 inches deep. This calls for filling the rest of the depth with another material. (Totally filling it with earth can make the base very heavy.)

Sheet styrofoam makes an excellent subsoil layer on which the sand or soil is spread, and serves to provide insulation against chill from beneath. Many florist supply stores or suppliers of plastic materials stock sheet styrofoam in varying thicknesses. Since soil depth need not exceed 2 inches, and sand or gravel need be only a half-inch deep, you should place slabs of tight-fitting styrofoam into the empty base on which you can then place soil and sand or gravel to suit your plan. Where potted plants are to be located, holes can be cut in the sheet foam in which to fit the pots so they rest on the floor below.

Before setting the styrofoam sheets in the base, slash grooves into the bottom surfaces and up the sides of the slabs of styrofoam so that air from the holes in the terrarium floor can be channeled to many points in the subfloor area.

Once the styrofoam is in place, and potted plants are in cut-out holes, soil and sand or gravel can be placed in the base on top of the styrofoam — soil in the deeper parts, sand and gravel in shallow areas. Soil should be spread around the pots to hide their rims. Rocks can also be used for this purpose. Both the earth and sand should come to about a ¼″ below the wood edges of the base. To keep soil from being tracked up on the side panels by animal life in the terrarium, a 2-inch wide layer of aquarium gravel should be placed on the surface of the soil next to the baseboards.

If a fountain or other water flow is included, space must be provided for its parts — particularly those that are unsightly. Fountain pumps can be used, but must of course be hidden from view if you wish the terrarium to appear natural. Most water fountains will need a subsurface water reservoir with connecting tubing along with a power source. Space must be planned for these components — usually in the subsurface styrofoam layer. Switches and water input tubes for these components should be recessed in the wooden base where they are handy, so the water display can be turned on or topped up with water without having to open the terrarium.

Refinements such as these should be well thought out before construction begins. If only anoles are to live in the shrubs grown in the terrarium, a water container is not needed: Anoles get all the water they need by lapping up moisture sprayed on leaves or condensation from the glass sides. If you plan to add a couple of infant box turtles to the terrarium, however, a source of drinking water will be needed, and will justify building an attractive running water display — perhaps even with a small filter to keep it clean! But whatever assembly you build, test it for a while outside the terrarium *before* you install it in the earthworks of your terrarium. Simple matters like leaky tubing, faulty pump, poor wiring and the like are easily corrected on a shop table, but are hard to deal with in the terrarium without disturbing it.

*The tabletop terrarium requires a framework which can be made of wood, glass, and aluminum. The framework makes a good shop-class project.*

*Construct one of the glass sides so that it will slide up, giving access to the case.*

*Four-inch-thick styrofoam forms the base, with holes cut into it to accommodate the largest plants.*

*Place gravel on the styrofoam to form a subsoil, and then begin to plant the smaller plants.*

70

Life in this kind of terrarium will require varying amounts of attention on your part, depending upon how complex the system is, but it should be of one kind: you need only *add* things — food and water — from time to time. If the plantlife grows well in the light provided by the special lights, if the soil is moist but not wet, if there are not too many animals — you should not have to clean up after them — then you will have created a fairly sophisticated yet functioning environment of living things in reasonable ecological balance. This is a system that lends itself to increasing sophistication. As you learn of its needs for improvement or you wish to expand upon its possibilities and increase your own experience by adding to its spectrum of living things, you can make changes in its functions.

Some animals like to bask in warm sunlight. In the terrarium this is accomplished by providing a tungsten lamp. You can create any warmth output you wish by providing a dimmer-control unit from a hardware shop that will vary the light intensity.

An air blower can be wired in to move air about in the terrarium or to exhaust it at any rate you decide by varying an in-out shutter blade. (This must be screened, of course, so that anoles do not get into it!)

In short: This is a system that can meet the needs of the most exacting home enthusiast or student of ecology. While it is a simple system, after the fashion of the original Wardian case, it is one that can be changed or added to, to meet almost any special need. In this system, environmental control is available to as high a degree as is possible outside a laboratory. The terrarium shown in the illustrations has reared several generations of a number of species of anoles. They bred and reproduced, laying their eggs in the terrarium soil. There is nothing static in such a terrarium. Those who peer into it will be confronted by a different scene each time they do so.

71

A terrarium can be created in almost any container you chance upon — and placed anywhere you feel it will be enjoyed the most. The systems we have discussed are ones you can build from the ground up or in unusual choices of commercial low-cost containers. The range of life that can be kept in different kinds of terrariums is quite large: from a plant in a simple bottle, to a Wardian case created in a plastic covered breezeway of a school — with entrances made from clear plastic film mounted in patio "screen" door frames! The possibilities are limited only by what you have yet to learn about living things, and your own imagination.

## Collecting Materials
## to Put in a Terrarium

The materials list cites a number of sources of wild plant materials and seeds, but part of the enjoyment of making a terrarium is going on field trips to collect your own plants.

Finding suitable plants does not always mean making a trip to some faraway forest. You would be surprised at what you can often find right near your own home. In the biggest of cities mosses can be found growing in the cracks of heavily traveled sidewalks and in the brickwork of walls.

Collecting plants calls for a few useful tools and something in which to transport the plants you have selected. One of the most useful tools

for gently digging up small plants from soil or the cracks in rocks is an artist's paint spatula. If you sharpen one edge of it, it will serve ideally to mark out, slice, and lift up a sample of moss bank from its place on the forest floor. Being flexible, it can cut in a curved shape, or bend to fit the shape of a rock ledge while you are trying to extract a plant without hurting its roots.

Ideal containers for organizing plant samples are small paper cups, and plastic sandwich bags are fine for storing slices of moss banks.

A plastic bucket is usually the best available container for carrying cups and bags of samples. Care must be taken, however, not to stack the cups in a way that will crush the leaves of the plants in them. It is best to pinch closed and fold over the top of each cup so that they can be loosely stacked in the carrying bucket without hazard to each cup's sample. Bags of moss can be stacked, but not too deeply. If you collect attractive slabs of rock you stumble on while collecting plants, put these in the bottom of the bucket even if this requires unpacking everything to do so — or carry a spare bucket for rock samples.

Surplus military canvas haversacks make ideal shoulder-strap carrying bags for rocks and plants. If you are collecting just a few plants, fishermen's bait boxes are handy field trip containers. Vlchek Plastics (see materials list) makes one of plastic that clips onto your belt. Complete with belt lugs, several of these around your waist will free your hands for other purposes.

Collecting plants in the woods should be done with care. First of all, you should ask permission of the owner. Whoever owns the land will welcome you back if you do not do too much harm while collecting plants. And if you are on public land, permission is usually needed to remove plantlife.

When you stumble on a fine cluster of mosses or other plants, try not to overcollect from any one spot. A good rule of thumb is to

74

75

remove only a fifth of any patch of moss, and only a plant or two from a cluster. By leaving most of any one cluster of plants, the spaces you have left will be filled fairly quickly with regrowth from the surrounding life. And always dig out — do not pluck — the plants you want, for most root structures are easily damaged by just pulling them out of the earth.

Aside from enjoyment, the field trip is an important part of the learning process. It is here that you first become aware of how many kinds of plants live together in one place, and experience firsthand the conditions under which they live. The trip will not, of course, be a substitute for further study about the matter, but it will provide a valuable personal insight into the things you will study later. As you read about the kinds of plantlife you collected or saw — and the animal life that was nearby — you will find it easier to understand and to appreciate the needs of these living things when they are transplanted into their terrarium "home, away from home" in *your* home — because you were there, in *their* home.

# Bibliography

Andrews, Mildred. *Gardens in Glass.* ———— A. T. De La Mare, 1934.

Baur, Robert. *Gardens in Glass Containers.* New York: Hearthside Press, 1970.

Grant, A. J. *Mosses with a Hand Lens.* Hamden, Conn.: Shoestring Press, 1924.

Green, Miriam. *Science-Hobby Book of Terrariums.* Minneapolis: Lerner Publishing Co., 1968.

Kramer, Jack. *Gardens Under Glass.* New York: Simon & Schuster, 1969.

————. *Rare Orchids Everyone Can Grow.* Garden City, N.Y.: Doubleday, 1968.

McDonald, Elvin. *Miniature Plants.* Princeton, N.J.: D. Van Nostrand, 1962.

Shuttleworth, Floyd and Herbert Zim. *Non-Flowering Plants.* New York: Golden Press, 1967.

Ward, Nathaniel. *On the Growth of Plants in Closely Glazed Cases.* London: John Van Voorst, 1842.

Zim, Herbert and Alexander Martin. *Flowers.* New York: Golden Press, 1950.

*Miniature Environments — An Environmental Education Guidebook* (Department of the Interior) Washington, D.C.: Government Printing Office. Publication #908-688 (price 25¢).

# Materials List

| ITEM | DESCRIPTION | CATALOGUE OR MODEL # | SOURCE |
|---|---|---|---|
| *Living items* | | | |
| Hermit crabs | Terrarium "housecleaners" — *dryland* variety only | LM491 | E. G. Steinhilber and Co. Oshkosh, Wisc. 54901 |
| Meal-worms | Food for animal life in terrarium | L 891 | Carolina Biological Supply Co. |
| Earth-worms | Medium size for frogs, turtles, etc. | L 408 | Burlington, N.C. 27215 |
| Plants and seeds | Tropical plants and orchids | | Alberts and Merekle Bros., Inc. Box 537 Boynton Beach, Fla. 33435 |
| | Woodland and bog plants | | Arthur Allgrove 279 Wilburn Street N. Wilmington, Mass. 01888 |
| | Desert and prairie plants | | Johnson Cactus Gardens Paramount, Calif. 90723 |
| | Desert and prairie seeds | | Prairie Gem Ranch Smithwick, S. D. 57782 |
| *Nonliving containers* | | | |
| Boxes | Plastic; all shapes for building moss ledges, small pots, construction, etc. (Catalogue includes hemisphere domes) | | Mail Order Plastics 58 Lispenard Street New York, N.Y. 10013 |
| Domes | | | |
| Boxes | Wide assortment of plastic containers | | Tri-State Plastic Molding Co. Box 337 Henderson, Ky. 42420 |

| ITEM | DESCRIPTION | CATALOGUE OR MODEL # | SOURCE |
|------|-------------|---------------------|--------|
| Domes | Restaurant food service plastic covers and matching trays | | Mastercraft Medical and Industrial Corp. 15-35 126th Street College Point, N.Y. 11356 |
| Domes | Acrylic domes | | Edmund Scientific Co. Barrington, N.J. 08007 |
| Film | For "blow-your-own-domes" system • "Butyrate" for best clarity • "Vinyl," rigid, for general use Butyrate blows at ±220°F, Vinyl at ±150°F | .015″ "15 mil" | Made by Flex-O-Glass, Tenneco, Eastman, etc. available small lots from many plastics distributors |
| *Support equipment* | | | |
| Blowers | Small cooling motor with 4-inch fan | #101 | Edmund Scientific Co. *See above* |
| | Several sizes of fans | | Lafayette Radio 111 Jericho Turnpike Syosset, L.I., N.Y. 11791 |
| Pumps | Waterfalls, fountains, filtration, etc. Along-the-line type — 15 gph, 25 gph, 38 gph | CAP5/1U CAP5/3U CAP5/7U | Fountains for the Home 2921 North 24th Street Arlington, Va. 22207 |
| Pumps | Fountain version; can be bulkhead mounted through bottom or side of containers | 60,803 | *Same as above* and: Edmund Scientific Co. *See above* |
| Thermometers | For control of temperature needs in temperature-sensitive situations — Dial, Bulb | 40,989 60,504 | Edmund Scientific Co. *See above* |

| ITEM | DESCRIPTION | CATALOGUE OR MODEL # | SOURCE |
|---|---|---|---|
| Water bottles | For plant care: stream feed | WB108 SB108 | Mail Order Plastics *See above* |
| Plant growth lamps | "Gro-Lux" fluorescent plant growth lamps | | Silvania Lighting Center Danvers, Mass. 44112 |
| | "Sun Bowl" — ideal for enclosing to create humid lighted enclosure for both plants and anoles | 69088 | Geo. W. Park Seed Co. P.O. Box 31, Greenwood, South Carolina 29646 |
| Lazy susans | Bases for construction of worlds under domes and other terrariums that need rotation | | Rubbermaid Product; in most hardware stores |
| Plant carrying box | With belt loops for carrying on waist Intended for fishing worms | V661 | Fishing stores or Vlchek Plastics Middlefield, Ohio 44062 |
| *Building materials* | | | |
| Angle aluminum | For construction of large cases | 2420 | Reynold's Aluminum (local stores) |
| Silastic rubber | Joining rocks in worlds under domes, and miscellaneous construction tasks | 9-80832 RTV-732 | Sears Roebuck Dow Corning in local stores |
| Epoxy film | "Five-Minute Epoxy" for rapid cementing For large walk-in "greenhouse" size terrariums, school breezeways, etc. | 6-10 mil Surlyn 1601-A | Local stores DuPont outlets |

# Index

87

## About the Author

John Hoke majored in biology at Antioch College. He has special interest in wildlife and photography, and often combines the two interests in his books. He is currently working with the National Park Services on projects to improve urban environments by restoring natural elements to our cities. Mr. Hoke's other books include *Ecology, Photography, Solar Energy,* and *Turtles and Their Care.*